Also in English by Reijo Rüster:
The Outer Isles 1982
In Swedish:
Den stora kappseglingen   1968
Kamera ombord   1970
Galjonsbilder   1975
Utskär   1980
Stockholm Öarnas Stad   1982

The idea for this book was suggested by Reijo Rüster, who has also taken all the photographs (apart from that on p. 117 showing a submarine surfacing in the middle of an armada of pleasure craft, which we have borrowed from Wyn Enqvist of the Information Dept., Swedish Naval Staff). Stig Tjernquist and Rolf Hellgren have been responsible for Art Design, in collaboration with Reijo Rüster. Graphic Design by Rolf Hellgren, assisted by Liz Elfgren. Ten different authors have lent their personal touch to the various chapters. The body of the text is set in Century Old Style, by Typografen 1. Captions in Century Old Style Light SC, by Typografen 2. Lithographic work by KåPe-Grafiska. The book is printed by Stellan Ståls Tryckerier, on 150 g Off Blade. Bookbinding by Bok-Lundins. Published by Stig Tjernquist Annonsbyrå AB.

ISBN 91-7260-847-1.

Tjernquist/83

STOCKHOLM CITY OF ISLANDS

REIJO RÜSTER

Translated from the Swedish by Keith Bradfield, Exportspråkgruppen

TJERNQUIST

CONTENTS

TO INGER Z. AND JERRY B.

PREFACE

From my window in Söder I look down towards Skeppsbron, the Räntmästar Steps, the Djurgården ferries, and a narrow sliver of the Baltic Sea.

In the old days, when the ships from Finland still moored at the quay in the Old Town, I used to hear their hoarse signals at 8 every morning as they passed Waldemarsudde on their way in. I could set my watch by them, and I learned to recognize their individual sounds: Svea Jarl, Wellamo, Ilmatar, the Bora boats...

On my way to and from my studio in the Old Town, I pass Slussen. From there it is so close to "French Bay" and the "England Quay" that I have taken them for granted, and thought very little about their history.

Having left the island of Södermalm, I find myself on another – "Stadsholmen", or the Old Town. From this, the centremost of all the islands, it is easy to reach Riddarholmen and Helgeandsholmen.

In this kingdom of islands, whose centre is around the Old Town, the archipelago extends out via Skeppsholmen, Kastellholmen and Beckholmen, to Fjärderholmarna. Islands and skerries crowd the horizon in every direction: Långholmen – known as the "Green Island" Reimersholme, Kungsholmen, and the islands of Årsta and Essinge. Some of them have been silted in to become part of the mainland, others are connected by bridges; several, however, are still accessible only by boat.

I find myself in the archipelago, in a world of islands, and yet in the heart of a great city. Stockholm is really a "City of Islands", each of them offering a history, a wealth of motifs, sufficient to fill a whole book.

The idea for this book emerged gradually from my various assignments in and around the waters of Stockholm, and after several years' work I offer here my selection, which I hope will afford pleasure to all those who love Stockholm and its world of water.

Reijo Rüster

THE OLD TOWN AND RIDDARHOLMEN

The first Swedish poet of any importance to portray life in the Old Town was Carl Michael Bellman. His Epistle No. 33, to take just one example, describes how Mowitz (the main character) and his friends set off by boat to Djurgården, from the quay at Skeppsbron, a rumbustious and motley crew of herring-packers, milk-women, tailors, card sharps, customs spies, and musicians. "Sun blazing, bells ringing, drums thund'ring, banners flying, pikes all a-gleam; and the bellringer trills and tolls."

In our own day it is Evert Taube we think of in the alleyways of the Old Town, and at Den Gyldene Freden ("The Golden Peace"), the oldest inn in Sweden. (It opened in 1721.) So what is left for the

amateur to say of this heart of Stockholm, cherished and besung by such great poets over the years?

The word amateur, from the Latin "amo", implies not just a dilettante, but also someone who loves, a lover.

My love of the Old Town, and my allegiance to it, were something I long kept secret. Something I was ashamed of.

I was born there – in the late 20s – and at that time this was no cause to put on airs. For four years the world outside my home was the area around Köpmantorget. The view from my window took in Nötke's "St. George and the Dragon", the Pilsener drinkers who seemed to have established permanent domicile on the stone bench in front of the statue, and, in the background, Köpmangatan – "Merchant Street" – Stockholm's oldest street-name, dating from 1323.

My memories are vague, fragmentary. I need the assistance of smells, sounds, the recollections of older brothers and sisters, for images to come to life. Neither Bellman nor Taube jog my memory. But a few lines from Ivar Lo-Johansson's "The Stockholmer" will take me back fifty years in the space of seconds.

"The island of the Old Town contained a brew of contradictions. Primaeval odours rose from the sewer gratings. Down by the water there was a fragrance of tar, of the harbour. The steamers emitted a smell of cold steam. In among the alleyways lived a human conglomerate, with swarms of kids. Victrolas like overgrown pot-plants screamed from the open, slanting windows. A penny cinema was running a Wild Western. Dockers stood bargaining with chest-high matrons for illegal spirits, or more seldom love."

Today the "human conglomerate" is made up of tourists, the swarms of kids are classes of visiting schoolchildren. And if anyone is still ashamed of living in the Old Town, it is certainly not on the grounds of indigence. *cont'd page 11*

Riddarholmen (above), and to the right the Old Town, with Skeppsholmen.

*Skeppsbron, with its stat[ue]
of Gustavus III and
the Logård Steps.*

Such are my thoughts today as I saunter along Köpmangatan and Österlånggatan, as they wind their way along like the footpaths they once were.

Many years later I was to re-encounter the throng of humanity, the swarms of kids, the music blaring from open windows, and the primaeval odours. When I visited Rome, and the narrow streets of Trastevere. And I felt that I had come home. The Renaissance buildings of Rome were also something *déja vue*: I was seeing in them, once more, Tessin's and Oxenstierna's Royal Palace in Stockholm.

I put the Old Town at the top of my list once when I was to play guide to an old Italian friend, on his first visit to Stockholm. He came, he saw, and was pretty reserved about the whole thing. But this was just like home, in the mediaeval town where he was born in North Italy!

cont'd page 13

The morning ship from Finland, seen from Tullgränd.

An August night at Kornhamnstorg.

11

No, the new town was what he wanted. Those five gleaming excavation marks – the then newly built sky-scrapers by Sergels Torg – sent him into raptures.

As did Riddarholmen. Not for its monumental patrician palaces. What gripped him so deeply was the monumental emptiness. We walked around the island one warm but stormy autumn evening. The waters of Riddarfjärden were white with foam. The government offices were closed. We were the only people. The buildings looked like painted scenery. We were on a stage. What a place to produce theatre, what a setting for the world's classical drama.

And here, indeed, Strindberg was born. Riddarholm's most famous son, throughout the ages. With due respect to Royalty, and all those noble houses...

Britt Ågren

Left: The Old Town, or "Town Between the Bridges".

Below: The Göta Canal boat departs from Riddarholmen. A popular trip among visiting Swedish Americans.

KASTELLHOLMEN AND SKEPPSHOLMEN

The islands of Kastellholmen and Skeppsholmen, like two fair jewels, stud the waters that were once the main harbour of Stockholm. In summer, they are clad in lush foliage; in winter, they are often delineated in strict black-and-white; always, they are a charming reminder of the majestic archipelago landscape that frames the approaches to the capital, and affords us a unique Paradise for our leisure.

In the early 17th century the Royal Swedish Navy began to move here from nearby Blasieholmen, which at the time the Royal Ship Wasa was built bore the name of Skeppsholmen. For more than three centuries, the Royal Swedish Navy and its ships thus stamped the islands with their character. In 1953, the Swedish Parliament decided that Naval Base East should move from Skeppsholmen to the southern archipelago. The move has been made, but the Navy still retains premises on the islands.

However, other interests have long been eager to take over any abandoned barracks, office buildings, training facilities, and quarters that may offer themselves. Moderna Museet succeeded many years ago in occupying the area where the Naval Base's Drill School, gymnasium, and guardhouses once lay. Konsthögskolan (the Academy of Fine Arts), has acquired premises here, as have the Museum of Far Eastern Antiquities and the Museum of Architecture. It is difficult, however, to see why Moderna Museet should have landed up in this pronouncedly maritime environment: it would have fitted in far better in Kulturhuset on Sergels Torg, amid all the teeming life that modern art tries in various ways to mirror.

Wisdom, good fortune, or difficulties in providing better communications to the islands have saved them, so far, from any fatal exploitation. Early in this century the question was discussed, perfectly seriously, of building high-rise tenement buildings on these islands, to accommodate in all around 10,000 people! We venture to hope that our modern town planners and politicians will steward this unique feature of our townscape with the utmost care, and with a proper feeling for the maritime traditions that are such an integral feature of Skeppsholmen and Kastellholmen.

Bengt Ohrelius

14

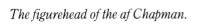

The battery on Skeppsholmen fires a 21 gun salute on the birthday of Crown Princess Victoria.

The figurehead of the af Chapman.

The craftsmen have returned to Skeppsholmen. "Squaresail House" with the chandler's, the sailmaking shop, and Pille the Rope-maker.

Bottom right: A reconstruction of the old derrick crane, dating from 1647.

In the reign of Oscar II, the Royal Swedish Yacht Club's (KSSS's) old clubhouse was used also as an ice-skating pavillion.

The place where the KSSS was founded is marked by a memorial stone.

Rowing practice on the Royal pinnace Vasaorden, designed by Chapman in 1774 for Gustavus III. The original pinnace was destroyed by fire; in 1922 a replica was built from the old, original drawings.

REIMERSHOLME

The last spirits have been distilled on Reimersholme. The old stills have been pulled down, and replaced by terraced, high-rise apartment blocks.

With the closure of the stills, after 108 years' production and handling of *brännvin* (aquavit), arrak punch, liqueurs, brandy and whisky, the final relic of an otherwise long outgrown era of Stockholm's history vanished: the close tie between factory and prison. Reimersholme has since been transformed into what is perhaps Stockholm's loveliest suburb – in the heart of the town. A very quiet upper middle-aged suburb it is, too, despite its two day nurseries. One of these is housed in Anders Reimers' former mansion: hatter, alderman and nature-lover Anders Reimers, who in the 1770s leased the greater part of Räkningeholm, as the island was then called, and built a magnificent summer residence there.

He was to be followed by other well-to-do gentlemen, who understood very well the art of combining business with pleasure. They

not only planted trees and constructed parks, as Reimers had, but started their own market gardens which produced a handsome profit.

Land on the island was very cheap, and labour was available not only close-to-hand but also practically free, at the prison on Långholmen. This combination proved irresistible. Soon, the greenery was replaced by factories, and by wretched, insufferably cramped, dank, ice-cold, workers' "barracks".

It was "Aquavit King" Lars Olsson Smith who made the name of Reimersholme famous. He took over a factory for the manufacture of "American kerosene oil" which had gone bankrupt, and started in 1869 a sophisticated distilling and purification plant for *brännvin*.

L. O. Smith believed in quick profits. Industrious, and in business matters utterly ruthless, he started a grand "aquavit war" against Stockholm's "Municipal Purveyor", a licensing system introduced with a view to damping slightly the enormous consumption of spirits. But Smith held the license on Reimersholme, which made him a popular figure indeed. He arranged free tours from Riddarholmen to Reimersholme and back by steamer, and no one travelled without a suitably large receptacle. On the island he sold "five-times-distilled pure aquavit" at a price of 1 krona 60 öre the jug (2.6 litres), a cut-price bargain even by contemporary standards.

The record was set the day (or rather day and night) that Smith kept four steamers going, leaving every twenty minutes with 25,000 passengers on board. The figure seems preposterous – one fifth of the entire population of Stockholm – but it has been authoritatively

cont'd page 24

Main picture, right: Evert Svedberg in the "spice loft", with the last sack of spice used on Reimersholme.
Above: The new apartments built by HSB, the Tenant-Owners' Association.

quoted by former Custodian of Antiquities Gösta Selling in his book "The Strange Destiny of the Mälar Queen".

The lady in question, with all her islands, has seen some goings-on in her day, but the figure quoted is probably ascribable to Smith himself, one of the sharpest marketing men of his day. In due course he was to seek – and make – his peace with the City of Stockholm, selling his by then run-down distillery to the Municipal Purveyor at an un-Christian profit.
An entrepreneur of spirit!

Dag Lindberg

Down in the dusky cellars of the distillery; the "Church", with its huge oak barrels for Grönstedts cognac.

Right: It was in 1977 that spirits finally ceased to flow under these attractive old lanterns, which are now preserved in a museum in Årstadal.

A big seller in its day was Kron-Brännvin.

THE ISLAND OF DESIRE

Here we sit, the two of us, on a sloping face of rock on Långholmen, near Västerbron (the "Western Bridge"), watching all the sailing craft and motor boats on their way to nowhere in particular. All of them, of course, have some sort of goal, but once that goal is reached they will start longing to move on. The busy searching here and there, for something else... What is this something else? The beauty of Nature? Freedom? Love? It is all this and something more.

Here I sit, close to my Woman, envying the boat-owners and their boats. While, they, perhaps, are envying us, as we sit here like Adam and Eve.

This whole island screams with longing. If all the shrieks of deprivation and hope that have been emitted from this island were collected on a tape, the resulting infernal howl would blot out the noise of the passenger planes that constantly pass overhead, to and from Bromma Airport.

And then, all the fighting men that have camped here over the centuries... Their battle cries; what were they but screams of fear in the face of death? A hope of escaping it; and of surviving to plunder and destroy. Engelbrekt, the revolutionary, stood on Långholmen in 1434 looking onto the city and lusting to take it; the hunger for power...

Ahlstedt, the brewer, built a palatial residence here in his desire to emulate the nobility, with their estates...

The graffiti and the nudes in the prison cells tell of the screams for freedom and love that have been hurled to the skies from the now demolished prison. "If this is life, death is nothing to fear." What remains of the prison is used by artists, striving for Perfection, for Beauty, for the oh-so-elusive Truth.

Now, in summer, one sees how many lonely people there are. They are lying around everywhere in an effort to acquire a tan; many of them also with a more or less conscious desire for "something to happen".

I sit beside my Woman and desire her, at the same time looking over the other women who pass by. And she? Perhaps, just now, she's thinking about some other man.

I jump into the water to cool off. I am hungry and thirsty. An eternal cycle, a longing for something: love, food, adventure, anything as long as life doesn't stand still. Although that, too, of course, we sometimes long for; that time should stand still. As at this moment on the sun-baked rock, if this moment could last for ever. If there could never more be winter and cold. And we could sit, through eternities, next to each other here on Långholmen.

Taisto Jalamo

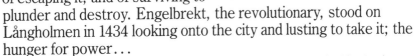

The picture left shows cell doors from the old Central Prison on Långholmen.
Above: Pålsundet in the spring.

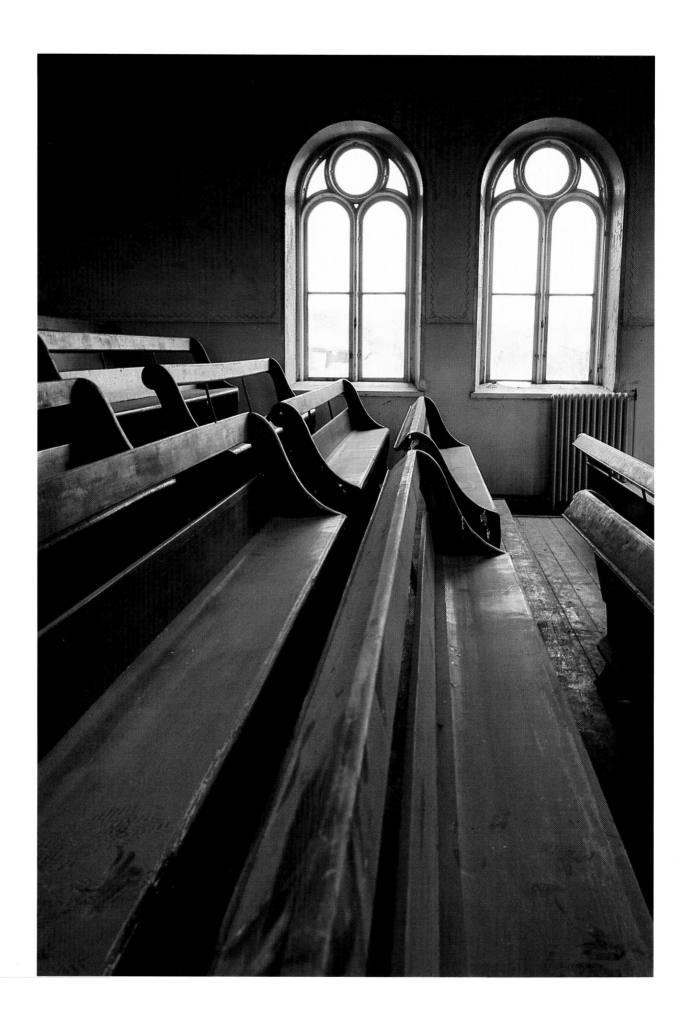

"My thanks to you, Långholmen!
You were so oft my precious home
From storms you were my haven
I think of you where'er I roam."

Interiors from the Långholmen Central Prison, now demolished. Parts of the prison have been preserved, and are used mainly by artists.

Left: The prison chapel.

LONG AFTER
THEY'VE GONE

The past, for today's people, had become a remote fairytale. That much he could gather as he sat down by the old jetty, listening to their conversation, and their fantasies about how things used to be in the old days here on his Fjäderholmar, or his "England" as he preferred to think of it, using the old name. (He was extremely conservative as regards the old names and customs.) Increasingly, he preferred to live with his memories. But it amused him to listen to people's speculations about life on the islands in the old days. Though he had to admit that he didn't understand the world of today. He simply could not stand, for example, those roaring plastic monsters that seemed every instant to be tearing past in the narrows between the

islands and Nacka. He remembered the men who used to put to at his jetty, men no longer among the living. He remembered their smacks loaded with salt Baltic herring and dried cod, with turnips and potatoes. You didn't see people like that, these days. What hands they used to have! Twice as broad as the pale, rake-like extremities people had today. And they smelled so good!

But most of all, if he was to be really honest with himself, he missed the fresh fish the smacks brought to him daily. They were wonderful fish, and the very thought of them made him drool with longing. Sometimes, it is true, he still got a few small perch from Inger, who apart from himself and Owl were now the only permanent residents on the island; but they weren't the same as the silvery night-fresh Baltic herring from Ingmarsö!.

There was, in fact, a great deal he missed. His nostalgia had actually reached the stage at which he missed the soldiers who had stored and manufactured their explosives deep under the rock. At least they had been organised and orderly. "You always knew where you had them," as he used to say to his friend Owl.

With a lump in his throat he would also tell Owl, who had moved to the islands fairly recently, of the days when there had been inns on the island. "There was no end to the amount of drinking and fighting and shouting that went on in the bushes round about." Owl used to listen eagerly to his risqué stories from this time. "You can't imagine how many girls and boys found each other in the flower meadow outside that old hovel – which in fact, in its day, was actually a public house, and a pretty lively one at that." The following day people would continue on their way to Harö or to Åland, or even further afield to Finland and Esthonia. "Sometimes in rowboats, all the way! What do you say to that, my feathered friend?"

He tended, also, to dwell at length on the restaurant of the bour-

cont'd page 36

The picture right shows the steps up to an old summer restaurant called the Belvedere, built in 1884. It burned down in 1940.

The Coastal Fleet passes Fjäderholmen.

Inger, who is warden of Fjäderholmen and its adjoining islands, is the only permanent inhabitant. From her house, she has a grand view of the main channel.

geoisie, the Belvedere, and its cuisine, describing in particular detail its halibut in white wine sauce. "But people were already getting a bit odd, and they had started drinking this sickly muck that sticks in your whiskers."

Owl and he used to end their nocturnal excursions on the steps of the old restaurant, where they could sit for hours peering out over the approaches. He would boast, on such occasions, that he was something of a walking maritime museum. He could remember practically all the different craft that had sailed past the island in his lifetime. And he would describe to Owl in detail the royal war ships, the galleys, the boyers, the galliots, the pinnaces, the fast-sailing smacks, crayers, prams, barges and other craft he had seen go past the island. But his eyes would close in pain when he saw one of the floating gin-palaces that now ply to Finland looming up behind Lidingö.

He had heard, recently, that people were now planning to clear his islands, and turn them into a sort of appendage to Djurgården, with paths, fruit-stalls and all manner of disciplined plagiarisms of Nature. "My time will soon be up, best strike the mainsail," he used to say to Owl.

If, as a nocturnal visitor to the island, you tread carefully, you can sometimes see a huge black old cat proceeding with dignity on stiff legs, tail erect between the luxuriant trees. Accompanied, always, by a younger, brown-speckled owl. They look as if they are talking to each other.

Taisto Jalamo

This house, once the local islanders' tavern, is well preserved. The jetty has long since been claimed by the ice, and only the abutments remain.

36

SWEDISH STEAM DAY

"Swedish Steam Day" is the popular label given to the grand "review" put on since the mid 1960s by the steamers plying in the Stockholm archipelago, on the first Wednesday in June each summer. The occasion's official designation is "Archipelago Boat Day", and it is arranged by the Archipelago Traffic Association in cooperation with the shipowners.

As island steamers are counted, naturally, also those plying between the islands in Lake Mälar. One of the most handsome vessels in this annual parade is thus the SS Mariefred, which has been plying the route between Stockholm and Mariefred since 1903. She is distinguished from the other vessels by her tall, plain black funnel, and by her bearing her name–painted in gold letters on her "chest".

The interesting thing is that these island-plying boats–those powered by steam–underwent a rebirth at the very instant in which they were about to die out. The great fleet of steamers that had sailed in the archipelago and on Lake Mälar since the turn of the century was

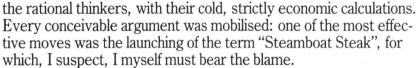

in the process, in the late 40s and early 50s, of being briskly scrapped.

The official policy on public transport was to extend land communications as far as possible by means of bridges and embankments. The rest was to be handled by ferries and tenders. On the longer routes, there was no longer any place for these large, comfortable vessels. At a time when practically all the steamers had disappeared, public opinion was suddenly aroused and the preservation was then fought against the rational thinkers, with their cold, strictly economic calculations. Every conceivable argument was mobilised: one of the most effective moves was the launching of the term "Steamboat Steak", for which, I suspect, I myself must bear the blame.

During the real era of the steamers, there was no such name. "Fried steak and onions" was all it said on the menu, insofar as this dish was on offer at all; nor was it surrounded by any particularly romantic aura. But for many of those concerned to save the steamers the phrase "Steamboat Steak", launched as it were almost posthumously, became something of a symbol for the now-lapsed and supremely desirable passenger traffic we wished to revive.

The campaign was successful, and it was a major achievement when Waxholmsbolaget–which was taken over in the early 50s by the County Council, and the public sector–decided to retain the steamers "Express II", "Norrskär", and "Storskär". The first of these was renamed the "Waxholm". This having been totally destroyed by fire one winter night some years ago, there remain only the "Norrskär" and the "Storskär", guarded now by public opinion as jealously as a dragon watches over a hoard of gold.

cont'd page 45

The steamers are all ready to put out from the quay in front of the Grand Hotel and Nationalmuseet. In the background Skeppsholmen, with Admiralty House and the full-rigger af Chapman.

The steamers set off from the Blasieholm quay, pass the Old Town, Skeppsholmen, Beckholmen and Waldemarsudde, continue past the beacon at Blockhusudden, and then head for Vaxholm.

The only steamer left plying in Lake Mälar was the "Mariefred". Its future was secured in 1966 when the Archipelago Boats Foundation acquired a majority shareholding in the company that owns it. Two years later the Strömma Canal company was formed, under whose red emblem two further steamers, "Drottningholm" and "Björkfjärden" now operate in Lake Mälar.

In Saltsjön the same company operates also the "Gustavsberg VII". In addition to which we have the stately "SS Blidösund", owned and operated by a large group of steamer enthusiasts.

This gives us a total of seven steam-powered passenger ships. Two of these, the "Mariefred" and the "Blidösund", are fired by coal. In the others, the water in the boilers is heated by means of oil.

This knowledge cannot, however, dispel my long-standing suspicion that these steamers are in fact fired by nothing less than steak... How otherwise is one to explain the intensive odour of fried steak–blended with fresh cucumber and the fragrance of dill in the potato pot–that permeates these vessels day in, day out, whether under way or at anchor?

This odour reaches its peak of intensity precisely on Swedish Steam Day, just before the steamers put out from Strömkajen, blending with the coal smoke that drifts in heavy clouds over Kungsträdgården. Then, as the steam whistles blast off together to signal departure, the people of Stockholm know that yet another summer season of steam has commenced.

What the new season will bring with it by way of encounters, adventures, and windy hours on deck, no one knows. But one thing is certain: the risk of going aground has been drastically reduced since the first shoal on the route–that which used to lie between Strömkajen and the Logård Steps–has been blasted away. This was done on Swedish Steam Day itself, and dead smelt and Baltic herring floated to the surface in their masses. The trip this June evening is to Waxholm and back; which is entirely in accordance with the old Swedish saying that if we meet no more in this life, we will always meet–in Waxholm.

Bo Grandien

Alongside the quays of Stockholm are moored many a West India-farer, many a vessel that has sailed the Seven Seas. They are house-boats now, some of them, for entire families, with children, dogs, and geraniums peeping out from cabin portholes.

The wheelhouse of one of these smacks is a sad repository for un-returnable empty bottles. The glass in a couple of the portholes is shattered. The table is awash with dried-up stumps of sausage, and with fag-ends by the hundred. Long-since wilted tulips droop over the edge of a paint tin; the instrument panel is stained with mustard and ketchup. The radio has been left on: "One–two–three, one–two–three, and so *roll* the trunk, one–two–three." From the stern hangs a large, ragged Swedish-Norwegian flag from the days of the Union. Amidships, between the fo'c'sle and the wheelhouse, is a tangled mass of life jackets, petrol cans, beer crates, dirty washing, and other unidentifiable garbage.

He bought this smack and moved on board when his wife divorced him. So, at least, it is rumoured among the regulars at Zum Franzis-kaner. Although it may, of course, have been the other way round…

Like everyone else in Stockholm, he has been waiting for the spring, and a new life. All his cold sorrows will evaporate in the warmth of the spring. His *angst* he will abandon on an ice floe, let-ting it drift out to sea on the melting ice, never to return.

He spends the entire morning making the vessel ready. He checks the fuel and the oil. He heaves the empty beer-crates up onto the quay, and cleans out the wheelhouse. He wipes off the instru-ment panel, and fixes the broken portholes with corrugated card-board. By 1 o'clock he is all ready. He's put on a clean shirt, and had a shave. He goes to the Coop up by the Katarina Elevator, and buys sausages and weak lager. Then he squints out over Saltsjön and beyond, towards the narrows between Djurgården and the Nacka mill. He looks over to the Stadsgården quay, and the herring fisher-men tugging regularly and monotonously on their lines. He sees the cars navigating the clover-leaf junction at Slussen; and his gaze sweeps over Skeppsbron, where two Russian passenger ships are moored. From the funnel of one of these, a faint plume of smoke is spreading out over Saltsjön. A miniature cloud hangs motionless over Skeppsholmen. Otherwise the sky over Stockholm today is blue as a meadow of cornflowers…

It is evening, late evening, at Zum Franziskaner. The place is filled with smoke, and the hum of voices. Sitting in the yellow light that surrounds the bar, he sees through the window how the black rock face of Katarinaberget merges increasingly with the approaching night. He looks out through the window, and tries from time to time to read the text on the windowpane: TNARUATSER.

He then goes on quietly to tell a politely attentive, uncomprehend-ing Japanese tourist all about the Vikings, the sea, and ships.

Down by the quay, his smack bobs gently in time with the waves. Up and down, up and down…

Each time a boat passes, his smack bobs with particular glee; its moorings creak, and he thinks that tomorrow by God he'll weigh an-chor and sail to Fjäderholmarna–or why not, dammit, all the way to Sandhamn!

Taisto Jalamo

Smacks lining the Strandvägen quay.

A summer night at the Strandvägen quay.

The Strandvägen quay looking towards Nybroviken, where the firewood and game merchants used to moor.

Norr Mälarstrand from the tower of the City Hall.

49

It's hard work refitting an old boat, but many of those you see obviously receive the most loving care and attention.

Houseboats and floating youth hostels lie side by side with the sand barges at Söder Mälarstrand.

THE RACE IN RIDDARFJÄRDEN

A faint smell of wool-fat and still waters spreads over the bathing-beach at Smedsudden. The closer you come to the starting-line, the more that of wool-fat prevails.

There they stand on the shore, immediately below the buildings housing Sweden's national newspapers, almost two hundred mountains of muscle. A throng of well-trained bodies, young competitive swimmers with bulging biceps and broad backs. And among them also quite a number of tanned, more elderly types. They grease their bodies, start warming up. One of them flaps his arms like a crow. Parents and trainers dart around, offering advice.

Suddenly I catch sight of her, a tiny lissom creature amid this throng of he-men. She is the one whose progress I will follow from the shore here to the City Hall!

The starter fires his gun. There is a violent splashing as they hurl themselves over the line into the deeper water, like a huge flock of startled eider. For a minute or so they appear to be swimming on each others' backs. I lose sight of my naiad immediately after the gun, but am confident of finding her again at the City Hall.

They round a buoy advertising an insurance company, and turn in the direction of the City Hall. By the time they reach Västerbron, the flock of eider has been drawn out into a long, splashing line. The wildly crawling competitive swimmers have taken the lead; well back in the field I spy an elderly gentleman proceeding now with the back-stroke, now with the breast-stroke. Riddarfjärden is quite choppy, the wind has blown up, and the pleasure boats are creating swells. The lifeboats lined up along Norr Mälarstrand add to the drama of the occasion.

The spectators have by now gathered along the quayside at the City Hall. Supporters, casual passers-by, all trying to stretch out over the railing to see past the smacks moored alongside the quay. Their necks grow longer and longer... The first swimmer should appear at any moment now. And there they come, two swimmers have drawn ahead of the field. A tough battle ensues between them. To the sound of lively encouragement, the Stockholm Police Force contendent pulls ahead fifty yards from the finish and wins by two lengths.

Only a few minutes later, the first woman competitor appears. She is well built, and suffering no apparent exhaustion. The others now appear in quick succession. Some seem disappointed, others are bright and cheerful; some are totally exhausted, a few look like drowned cats.

My slender naiad has still not appeared. More and more swimmers reach the finish... I remain for over an hour, waiting until the last swimmer has completed the course.

Did I quite simply miss her? Did she abandon the race? Or did she fail to start? Perhaps she was an optical illusion, a wishful thought, a dream.

Or perhaps she won't be starting until next year...

Stig Tjernquist

Length of course: 3,200 metres
Best time: approx. 33 minutes
Worst time: approx. 90 minutes

GONE FISHIN'...

Why do so many people fish from the quays of Stockholm, and from its bridges?

Because it's a convenient pastime. Because it's free. Because they like fish. Because they have a cat to feed. Because they're lonely. Because they want to be alone. Because they are hard up. Because they like the view. To sense the passage of time. Or to keep time from passing quite so fast... There are as many reasons for fishing as there are fishermen. The hard-up, those who fish to reduce their expenditure on food, foregather at Stadsgården, on the quay between the huge ferries to Finland and the icebreakers that have been laid up for the summer. These fishermen have simple gear consisting often just of a line with five shiny hooks and a sinker. Of all fishermen in the city, these are the people who get the best catches. Fat, glistening Baltic herring, sometimes by the bucketful. A divine justice here prevails, by which the poor receive most of what the sea has to offer. These herring fishermen are mostly from the heights of Southern Stockholm. They come down from the areas around Great Glassworks Street, from Vita Bergen (the "White Heights"), from Mosebacke. Mosebacke was known in the 17th century as Fisherman's Cliff, because that was where the seine fishermen lived. There is still a Fisherman's Walk there today.

The fast-flowing, turbulent waters around Helgeandsholmen, the island that houses both the Riksdag (the Swedish Parliament) and the Bank of Sweden, are among the best in Sweden for the amateur fisherman, but they are also tricky in the extreme. Many a lure has got snagged in the remains of the ring of stakes put down here to protect the city against the Danish King Kristian II in 1520. And the "Chronicles of Erik" mention this island in connection with the execution of King Birger's son Magnus, in 1318:

"To the Holy Isle they straight him ledde
A carpet fayre beneath him spredde;
There knelt he down, with royal mien as ever
There gav'st commande, his royal head to sever."

The right of Stockholmers freely to fish in these waters dates back to an age long vanished, namely to the reign of Queen Kristina in the 1650s; and the few seine fishermen still to be found in Norrström are the heirs of fellow seiners from the early Middle Ages.

But today's fishermen use sophisticated modern equipment to get the salmon and salmon-trout to rise. The record to date appears to be a giant of 14 kilos, landed just below Strömparterren.

Anyone wanting to fish in peace, away from the onlookers, the traffic, and the parading soldiers, has not all that far to go; he simply strolls past Nationalmuseet, on Blasieholmen, and crosses to Skeppsholmen and Kastellholmen, where the fishing may not be as good as between Riksbron and Strömbron, but where he can delight instead in the gurgling of the water between the cracks in the old stone quay, and the sighing of the wind in the trees. But fishermen here must always beware of getting their lines caught on the bottom! Because this much is certain: the fishing may be as good here as in the nightly rivers in the north; but on the sea bed practically anything may be lurking, having drifted here, been dumped here, or sunk here. Stockholm, after all, has been standing by these waters for over seven centuries.

Taisto Jalamo

Stocking with fish fry at Skeppsholmen.

The picture left shows the Swedish Navy's training schooner Falken, which holds up the fishing for a few minutes.

You can catch more than just herring in the waters of Stockholm: pike, eel, burbot, grayling, salmon trout, salmon, bleak, ide, pike-perch, Cyprian carp, bream, roach, stickleback, catfish...

A recipe for Baltic herring, from southern Stockholm:
Clean the fish, and turn it in a mixture of white pepper, salt, egg and wheat bran
(or bread crumbs).
Place the fish in a greased baking dish, and stuff them with chopped parsely and
small, thin slices of garlic.
Arrange "thumbnail-thin" slices of carrot around the dish in a garland.
Garnish with whole cloves of garlic, to perfect the arrangement.
Cook in the oven at approx. 200°C.
Serve when golden brown with fresh boiled potatoes and a well-chilled dry white
wine.
Or with cellar-cooled beer...

The picture at right shows one of the dip-net fishermen who have for so long been
a popular sight on the waters of Stockholm.

Frogmen from the Coast Artillery demonstrate the sort of things they find when
cleaning up the sea bed.

"THE STRÖMMEN DIPPERS"

Who can fail to be impressed by all the sporting activities that go on in Stockholm? In the heart of the metropolis, without even having to stump up the price of a ticket, you can join the spectators at the Sail Day races, the swimming in Riddarfjärden, and that major international event, the Stockholm Marathon – to mention only a few of the main fixtures. You can also watch all the young people who play football, ice-hockey and tennis, urged on by enthusiastic parents, in the hope perhaps that their own particular offspring will be a new Ralf Edström, a new Anders Hedberg, or even a new Björn Borg. You will further observe a large and exuberant troop of amateurs practising their sport in the spirit of the current fashion of jogging: people walking, jogging, running and bicycling, their aim perhaps nothing

more than to beat yesterday's time to or from work.

One new sport now on offer is white-water kayaking in Stockholms Ström, the home waters of Stockholm's only club devoted to this purpose, the "Strömmen Dippers", formed in 1978. Although world championships have been arranged since 1949, white-water kayaking did not really gain a foothold in Sweden until quite recently. A kayak slalom was included in the Olympics in Munich, and the sport is well-established internationally. Perhaps the best way of describing it is to compare it with skiing. An event is either slalom or "downhill". A slalom course should be about 800 metres in length, and include twenty-eight gates: in Strömmen, the course is necessarily somewhat shorter; but you need a steady nerve even in these "easy" waters. The "downhill" race is in wilder waters: the course is a long one, and participants are free to choose their own route. The current should be really strong, with a few extra challenging stretches of rapids. White-water kayaking is a "tough" sport, but actual injuries are rare. Tommy Landén, an ardent enthusiast, tells us that the worst accident in Stockholm to date has been the loss of a front tooth. Life jackets, of course, are compulsory.

By tradition, the "Dippers" hold their white-water kayaking race on the last Saturday in April. We can only hope that both the race and the sport are here to stay. And who knows, if the Dippers produce their own Ingemar Stenmark, the sport may one day be as big in Sweden as Alpine skiing.

Stig Tjernquist

Kayakers preparing for the start, in front of the Royal Palace. The picture left shows white-water kayakers at one of the last gates before the finishing line. In the background, spectators on Norrbro.

THE SEAPORT

The waters of central Stockholm today bear witness to a special sort of affluence. The tonnage lined up along the quays is now, almost without exception, designed to meet people's need of recreation. The island steamers herd together in front of the Grand Hotel and Nationalmuseet, at the foot of Slottsbacken, and in the heart of Nybroviken. Long, low sightseeing craft lie at anchor beside Strömbron. The Viking Line's red ferries to Finland have their terminal at the Stadsgården quay, while the Åland Line's "Princessan" tempts us to frivolous jaunts across the Sea of Åland from its berth by Slussen. During the months when there is no ice, the state's fleet of icebreakers also holes up at Stadsgården and awaits events, practically the only evidence in sight of the more serious type of shipping

on which we in Sweden, in fact, depend. The last relics of a once extensive traffic in general cargoes, by coastal and North Sea vessels, vanished from Stadsgården in the 60s; at roughly the same time, the last white, oceangoing passenger ships left their berths at Skeppsbron.

On the north-western tip of Djurgården, where the naval dockyard used to operate, there is now a marina for 220 visiting pleasure craft. Outside the Galärvarvet dock are moored the former icebreaker "Sankt Erik" and the Finngrundet lighthouse, both now museum pieces. Otherwise this quondam workplace has been transformed into a lawned and patched recreational area.

Along Strandvägen, where smacks from the archipelago, and from Åland, once discharged timber, sand, and other goods, now lie row upon row of old vessels in various degrees of preservation, but all the objects of loving care on the part of their owners.

Through the Karl Johan lock pass in summertime a string of attractive pleasure craft on their way from the fresh to the salt water, or vice versa.

The winds of change have swept the "real" shipping from Stockholm's central waterways. This, however, does not mean that Stockholm has ceased to exist as a shipping centre. The Port of Stockholm handles some six million tons of goods per year. In the Stockholm archipelago, commercial shipping accounts for some thirteen thousand "ship movements" per year, the emphasis being on ferries, with their cargoes of passengers, passenger cars, and trucks.

Modern cargo handling requires a lot of space, and it has been found necessary to concentrate most of the sea-borne goods traffic to Värtahamnen, and to the city's specialised oil harbours. Lindarängen – in the 20s Sweden's first real airport, with services to Finland and Germany – became in 1971 the first container terminal on the country's east coast. It is still the only terminal of its kind on this side of Sweden. In the space of a few decades, life in the Port of Stockholm has been completely transformed by larger vessels and modern cargo handling, with unit cargoes, containers, and roll-on roll-off. The inner city's numerous long quays, once dominated by the stevedores, the busy cranes, and the cargo ships, have become promenades, parking lots, and temporary berths for pleasure craft of all sizes.

Bengt Ohrelius

Stadsgården quay from the Katarina Elevator.

Uno Andersson, who has worked in the free port since 1945, supervises the unloading of coffee from Brazil.

The only container terminal on the Swedish east coast is at Värtan. In the 1920s, seaplane services were started here, to carry passengers to Finland and Germany.

Bottom left: The old hoisting cranes in the free port.

The Navy and the Port of Stockholm collaborate in a sea-rescue exercise off Kastellholmen.

The OK company's 35,000-tonner
in the narrow oil harbour at
Ryssviken.

Fishing in Hammarby Harbour.

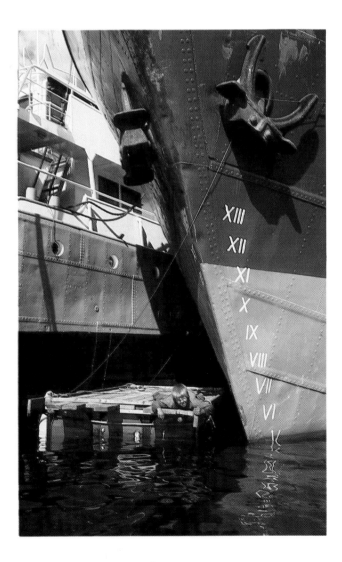

The morning ship from Helsinki arrives at the
Finland Terminal in Värtan.

Boats from Lake Mälaren tied up at Klara Mälarstrand.

The Viking Line's Finland Terminal below Fåfängan. These red ships ply to Åland, Åbo and Helsinki.

THE HARBOUR OARSMAN

"Our job has its risks. I remember rowing down from Slussen one winter day, in a strong stern wind, to pick up a pilot and put him on board a German ship. I came alongside and got a line thrown down into the skiff. I took a turn round the forward bitt, paid out the line to bring us below the ladder, and the pilot climbed abroad. I stayed hauled alongside until we were approaching the quay, and then I climbed aft. The sea was rough, the wind was directly over the bow, and the German put on a surge of speed. I heard a crash, and the bitt and the stem of my skiff were torn right off. I jumped forward and grabbed the ladder with one hand as the skiff went down. And so I was dragged in the water, alongside the ship, from Fåfängan almost half way up the Stadsgården quay. There was drift-ice around, but luckily the floes hit the stem of the ship, not me. As we came closer to the quay people were calling out:'Can't you see there's a man in the water alongside you?' Then a mate came down the ladder, and I was helped on board. When I got ashore I was so frozen and covered in ice I could scarcely walk."

From the notes jotted down by a harbour oarsman in 1919... And that was the sort of thing that could happen. The first motor-powered dinghies came into operation in the early 1920s, but until then it was oars. And their successors are still proud to call themselves "harbour oarsmen". The job has long traditions. No one knows how far it dates back, but in all probability there have been harbour oarsmen in Stockholm for as long as there have been ships.

Before the days of motorboats, they used the capacious craft known as "ship brokers' dinghies", plus various easily handled small skiffs about four or five metres in length. These boats and their gear had to be sturdy: a thick cable or a wet hawser could be a pretty heavy load to row to the quay. And as sturdy as the boats were the oarsmen themselves, most of them experienced seamen who had tired of life at sea and signed on for shore duty. Men who knew the sea, and could speak the international language of seamen.

It was and still is the harbour oarsmen who first extend the hand of welcome to seafarers, on behalf of the Port and the City. They are on call day and night. In all weather, and in all seasons.

But, of course, the traffic today is not what it was, as harbour oarsman Gösta Jansson will tell you. He first went to sea in 1934, and signed up as a harbour oarsman in the mid 50s. Just how many cables and hawsers Gösta Jansson has brought ashore and ferried out since then is anyone's guess.

But even if the harbour was livelier in the old days, and its waters bluer, it still exerts the same power of attraction over this splendid old-timer.

Ragnar Karlström

A ship in the process of being moored to a buoy in the road off the Stadsgården quay. Mooring at buoys is becoming increasingly infrequent; quay berths are preferred for economic reasons.

Harbour oarsmen Gösta Jansson and Artur Idman at work.

ANDERS THE WELDER

He'd begun at the yard more or less by chance. That first day when he walked in through the gates he could never have imagined that he would still be working there four years later. But he felt, somehow, that he just couldn't hand in his papers. Perhaps it was his mates, the comradeship, the pride they all felt in their work; or perhaps it was the threat of a shut-down, the feeling that it wasn't even going to be his own choice whether or not to go on working, that made his job with the yard seem so important.

Only a couple of hours left now, before the holiday he had been looking forward to so much. It made him feel a bit odd. The thoughts churned round in his head. He had promised them such a lot these past few months. Raising his family's expectations with dreams of a sailing-trip to Bornholm, or at least to Öland. That, he thought, was the least he should come up with to justify the interest payments on

his – to be honest – overly expensive boat. Though the salesman at the Boat Show had guaranteed that it was a good buy, and a safe investment given the deductible interest and rocketing boat prices.

"Unless Anders the Welder is right after all," he thought, and a shiver ran through his body. The way Anders had bloody gone on about a saturated market, falling prices, and his old wooden sailing boat that he'd bought outright for only twelve thousand.

A right know-all, Anders the Welder. Always knows the lot. I mean, think how he goes on about all the boatyards in Stockholm where he says he's worked.

And then there were Anders' jokes... Worst of all his boating stories, with all their cracks at people like himself who had fibreglass boats. "You can't compare a glass tub to a real boat, the only one getting any benefit out of that soap-dish of yours is the bank." And the way Anders the Welder would start off an ordinary Monday morning: "Well me old mates, my nose may be red, but don't think I've been hitting the bottle this week-end. I was caulking the old yacht, and caught the spring sun." The moment you heard "Well me old mates...", you knew what was coming. He'd keep it up until the 11 o'clock break. With stories of the old days, and all he'd done to safeguard the future of the yard. How he'd torn strips off both the politicians and the union bosses.

Of course, Anders knew his job. You had to admit that. If you ran into any difficulties at work, you could always ask Anders. He wasn't called Anders the Welder for nothing. You'd be hard put to it to find his match at spot welding.

"It's funny," he thought, as they walked out through the gates a couple of hours later. "At the end of the day we always march out in a little knot around Anders." He couldn't say why. And as they parted outside the gates he heard his own voice saying: "Have a great holiday, Anders. Lots of sun, and a good wind... And give my love to the family!"

Stig Tjernquist

Finnboda Shipyard, from Finnberget.

The Balder Dona has 25 metres added to her length at Finnboda Shipyard.

Beckholm Shipyard, Djurgården.

An icebreaker undergoes its annual check-up in the dry dock at Beckholm Shipyard.

Interior from the Mälar Yard.

A boat is made ready in the spring at Årsta Strand, at one of the many clubs in Stockholm for small boats.

The pictures above are from the Mälar Boatyard on Långholmen, which dates back to the 18th century.

A boat being launched against the background of the Wasa Museum, Djurgården.

THE CITY'S LOCKS

Stockholm is above all a city for boatmen. It always has been. It is built on islands, and boats have been the natural way of getting about. They still are, even if the emphasis is now more on pleasure than necessary transport. Just how many pleasure craft there are tied up along the shores of Stockholm no one really knows, but they can be measured in tens of thousands. There are superb natural harbours both in Saltsjön and Lake Mälar. Between these bodies of water are two constricted lines of communication, each a needle's eye: Slussen, in the heart of the city, and Hammarbyleden, just south of Söder.

In summer, Stockholm explodes in a mass of outdoor activities, ranging from music and theatre in the streets and squares to concerts, games and community singing in the parks and other gathering-places. One standing feature in this exuberant supply of entertainment is Slussen, where the most breathtaking and hilarious numbers are performed daily and hourly by the people in boats, themselves mostly unaware of the quality of their performance. In the course of a single summer over 30,000 boats pass through this needle's eye between Saltsjön and Lake Mälar, and the skipper of any small craft had better be on his toes when his turn comes: the crowds of spectators in the stands overlooking the lock chamber are waiting avidly for him to make a fool of himself.

The lockage is his moment of truth, or in many cases rather a purgatorial fire to be endured. The man steers, his woman crews for him and staves off the vessels jostling alongside. No-where else are their roles so clearly defined as here in Slussen. The whole core of the drama is the man's self-evident right to swear, rant and roar like the captain of some ancient full-rigger. His is the star-ring role, and it is for his entrance the spectators are waiting. Nor do they wait in vain. On a summer afternoon, the lock is packed with boats, all jostling together, impatient to get into the chamber and be sluiced out into the waters beyond. Minor crashes and collisions are inevitable. The little boat-owner in his dashing nautical cap suddenly becomes the great Captain Bligh, giving vent to his innate longing single-handedly to command the Seven Seas. But there are also plenty of experienced off-shore yachtsmen with similar urges in this little basin, which is suddenly transformed into an amphitheatre filled with hitherto unrevealed histrionic talent, acting out a brief melo-drama in which, as it culminates, are deployed body language, gestures, and an unfailing stream of lines packed with oaths and invective.

The lock gates open, and in a few minutes the melodrama is over. The chamber fills with a new armada of small boats. Enter new skippers. A new performance is about to begin. And no two of them are alike. And so the summer days pass on the most central outdoor

cont'd page 90

Left: The Hammarby lock. Above: The Karl Johan lock.

stage in Stockholm, where every performance is free. In Stockholm's other needle's eye, Hammarbyleden, things are a bit quieter. Here it is the big cargo ships that set the tone, and things proceed calmly and soberly. In summer, however, the pleasure craft dominate also in this lock, the only one capable of handling ocean-going ships from Saltsjön. Excavating and blasting were completed in the late 1920s, and since then this lock has been a vital link for the commercial traffic on Lake Mälar.

The lock between the Old Town and Söder, on the other hand, has been in existence for centuries, even if its actual construction has varied. At the beginning of time there was a natural stream here, linking Lake Mälar with Saltsjön, and the boats were

cont'd page 92

A sightseeing boat passes beneath the Underground line on its way to the Karl Johan lock.

winched upstream by hand.

In the mid-17th century, when skippers had been complaining for hundreds of years about this scarcely navigable channel, the first lock was finally built. Since then, new constructions have been regularly introduced at intervals of around 100 years. In 1750, the "Polhem lock" was built, to be followed in 1850 by the "Karl Johan lock". The latest major reconstruction in this century, in 1935, completely remodelled the area. The entire Slussen complex, with its roadways, walkways, train tracks, lifts, workshops, buildings and lock chamber is in fact a miniature technological wonder, which thanks to its ingenious construction successfully transports streams of people from Södermanland to Uppland and vice versa without traffic jams.

Ragnar Karlström

The statue of King Karl Johan, who gave his name to the lock. Pleasure craft on their way out from the city.

SAIL DAY

As you stand there on the quay jostling elbow-to-elbow with the crowds in the sunshine, watching hundreds of sailing craft – also jostling and crowding each other as they round a nearby buoy – it strikes you what a remarkable city Stockholm really is.

A city whose numerous waterways fill with sailing boats the first week-end in September each year, a city in whose centre sail racing has become a popular spectator sport.

And you think to yourself how beautiful it all is when these waters are filled with sail, and that it should always be like this.

The whole thing really began in 1923, with the inauguration of the City Hall. A Grand Regatta was held in Riddarfjärden, an event immortalised by artists and photographers. There had always, in fact, been sailing and racing in Riddarfjärden, but this Regatta was something special.

Then, some time during the 1960s, the gentlemen members of a newly formed and exclusive sailing club decided it would be a good thing to continue racing large yachts in "Riddarhavet", as they briskly renamed the water between Västerbron and Slussen. The club was, and still is, called – in English – the Gaff Yacht Society, and its stated purpose is to preserve old sailing boats and combat any tendencies to dullness and uniformity in the sport.

The GYS started to arrange races in Riddarfjärden every year, the first week-end in September. The main event was, and still is, the battle for a ghastly pot dubbed – again in English – "The Scandal Beauty Trophy".

These races became increasingly popular, and the arrangers were obliged to restrict entry so as not to fill Riddarfjärden with too many boats. Many yachtsmen were unable to take part, and they were naturally fed up about it.

And so one autumn day – it must have been a Thursday, as the menu consisted of the traditional pea soup and arrak punch – a number of gentlemen who comprised the GYS Riddarfjärden Committee were holding a "planning meeting" in Saltsjö-Duvnäs, when one of them – in fact it was GYS Chairman Per Olof Brandt – burst out: "But for heaven's sake, the answer is to have sailing on all the waters in Stockholm, what we need is a sort of 'Sail Day'!"

It was clear to those present that the little GYS, with its sixty members, could never cope with such a task, but a journalist who was present stood up. "Chaps! I'll have a word with the newspaper."

And his newspaper, Svenska Dagbladet, had people on the board who realised what could be made of this. And together with GYS and the Stockholm Yachting Club, the chairman of which was former Star class champion Lasse Löfgren, Svenska Dagbladet arranged the first Sail Day on 7 and 8 September 1974.

No one knew for certain how many boats would turn out on the 11 different courses all over the city, and applications were slow at first to come in; but when it was time to start them off, Jacques Nyman, as "general in charge", could count up to a thousand.

According to the police, there were half a million people on the quays watching. Information and commentaries were relayed over loudspeakers.

cont'd page 103

A jostle of boats rounding the buoy off Långholmen. In the background, Västerbron and Marieberg, with its newspaper offices.
Overleaf: Boats moored alongside the City Hall.

It is not only your standard modern racing boats that turn up on Sail Day. Some remarkable craft are to be seen. Although the Regatta is held in the heart of the city, a squall can blow up, catching yachtsmen by surprise.

start, helping to arrange this huge folk festival of sailing, the biggest "sails promotion" ever, and still more are now joining in.

The best view of all is perhaps from the Riddarholmen terrace, which troubadour Evert Taube considered the most beautiful spot in all Stockholm. And from there, with luck, you can see some of the "greyhounds of the sea" that took part in the first Regatta on Riddarfjärden in 1923.

Lars Porne

Sailing boats heading for the buoy in front of the Old Town Underground Station.

Being a conversation between an *Optimist* and a Pessimist on a bench overlooking the Djurgården Canal one sunny day, the week before Midsummer, in the early 1980s...

– What a splendid day, what a delight to see all these people enjoying life, and enjoying the sun that has come to thaw us out after a dreadful winter.

– *Without a thought, any of them, to the transitory nature of such moments!*

– And just look at all those joggers and horsemen–and horsewomen!

– *None of these sweating hearties has realised the vanity of trying to flee from the inevitable, they believe they are prolonging their lives, poor souls... That horsewoman there with the flowing hair lacks any sense of the invisible Horseman riding behind her...*

– Come on, cheer up. Remember that this was once reserved for the King and the Court, but today we can all enjoy this oasis.

– *And where, pray, are all those who once flaunted their clanging spurs and finery here? Dust!*

– Can't you see Love pulsating in the hearts of these young people? Look at those loving couples, seeking out a place where they will be undisturbed.

– *The love urge is also a death wish of sorts...*

You're hopeless, can't you see all the beauty around you, look at the water of the canal, it's like a mirror, and look at those stately villas up to Rosenhill.

– *Where the rich continue to live as if they thought there were pockets in shrouds...*

– What about a spot of this vintage claret?

– *The consumption of spiritous liquors in public places is prohibited by law.*

– Who the hell cares?

– *Probably those police officers you see approaching.*

– Then let us stroll down to the Djurgården Inn, and take a glass there.

– *"Today sees you merry and red, tomorrow you'll be pale and dead."*

– Seriously, what's making you so gloomy? You don't usually talk this way in the pubs in town...

– *The passage of time is so tangible here, the wings of history make their presence felt more than anywhere else in Stockholm.*

– Would it help if I sang a few lines of Bellman?

– *Why not "Drink deep your glass! See there, how death awaits you"?*

– Shall we take the bus back to town?

– *They're all packed with howling kids and hysterical mothers!*

– A taxi?

cont'd page 111

Right: One of the old Djurgården ferries, now deployed only in the peak tourist season. Overleaf: Sun worshippers along the Djurgården Canal.

The Djurgården Canal and its banks are an oasis for many Stockholmers. Here one sees casual strollers, sunbathers, fishermen, people rowing, people in sailing boats and motor launches...

The clubhouse of the Stockholm Rowing Club.

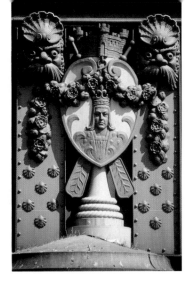

A decorated detail on Djurgården Bridge, designed by Erik Josephson. The bridge was opened in 1895, the year of the Stockholm Exhibition.

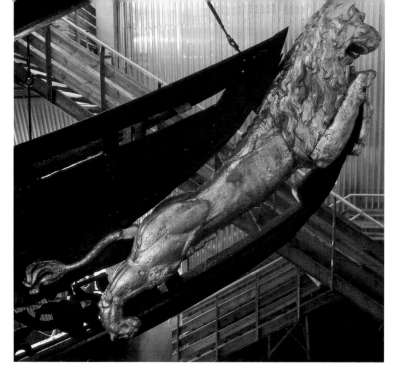

The figurehead of the warship Wasa. The Wasa Museum is neighbour to Gröna Lund, Stockholm's summer funfair.

The National Maritime Museum runs courses in practical seamanship every year for the youth in Stockholm.

– "Stockholm Taxi, answering service… Your call will soon be connected, estimated waiting time something under five years…"

– You really are the end, but I'm not going to let a wet blanket like you ruin my day. I mean, why do you bother to come here?

– Because it's all so bloody beautiful! Shall we not stroll in the shadow of those oaks, along to Blå Porten for some refreshment?

– You're on!

Taisto Jalamo

The figurehead of Gustavus III's pinnace Galten ("The Boar"), carved by Johan Törnström. Both the figurehead and the pinnace can be seen at the National Maritime Museum (Sjöhistoriska Muséet).

Every year the Swedish capital is visited by numerous cruising ships, carrying tourists from near and far. A ship will put in for a day or so, or sometimes only for a few hours, dropping its passengers for a sightseeing tour and some shopping. In the old days the great giants always lay at anchor out in Strömmen, moored to round red buoys, and admired at a distance by the youth of Stockholm, who would comment expertly on their funnel markings, their elegance of line, and their tonnage.

Now even the largest cruising ships glide at a gentle pace into Stadsgårdskajen, and some of the smaller go right in as far as Skeppsbron.

A vast company of sea-borne tourists travel every year with the Silja, Viking and Åland lines: some six million people commute annually between Stockholm, Åland and Finland on the red, white and blue-yellow-red ships of these companies. Many of them on a mini-holiday, dancing, eating, drinking or sleeping their way across the Sea of Åland, and through two of the loveliest archipelagoes in the world.

Naval visits are also among the more eye-catching elements in the busy life in and around Strömmen. Cruisers, destroyers, submarines, even aircraft carriers navigate their way gingerly through the tortuous approaches to Stockholm, to visit the city and rest up between periods of training at sea.

The salutes they fire echo off the rocky heights to the south, and receive a prompt reply from the guns at Kastellet.

In 1956 Queen Elizabeth II arrived on a State visit on board the Britannia, accompanied by an appropriate escort. King Fredrik of Denmark often used to come on his white yacht Dannebrog. Before the Second World War, the money magnates of the day were accustomed to go cruising on their own steam-yachts. These dazzling white apparitions, with their yellow funnels, sweeping lines, slim masts and bowsprits would anchor in Strömmen, or tie up in Nybroviken next to the Strand Hotel.

Strömmen and Riddarfjärden offer splendid stages for maritime spectacles, a fact of which the Swedish Navy has occasionally taken advantage. The year 1959 saw the first "Operation Strömmen" on a grand scale, with the participation of destroyers, MTBs, helicopters and submarines from the Coastal Fleet. The School of Navigation has held sea-rescue exercises there, and on a couple of occasions submarines have performed, above and below the surface of Strömmen.

Bengt Ohrelius

The submarine Sjöhunden at Skeppsbron, with the af Chapman, Admiralty House, and Skeppsholmen Church in the background.
The German Navy's training-ship Gorch Fock on her way into Stockholm.
Overleaf: Sails being furled on the Gorch Fock, against the background of the Katarina Church.

An Italian cruise liner passing Kastellholmen on her way out of Stockholm.

Submarine Day is another popular event in Strömmen. Among a whole armada of pleasure craft, a submarine surfaces a couple of hundred yards off Kastellholmen.

Passengers from the Greek cruise liner Royal Oddyssé buying Swedish crystal that has been laid out for their inspection on the quay.

Hundreds of lights, on board the Åland Line's Prinsessan, and the Visborg, the Coastal Fleet's commando ship, shine out in the summer night.

The Greek Navy's training ship, Aris, on a visit to Stockholm. The cadets are received by the city's representatives–both official and unofficial.

LUNCH ON BOARD

She was once called the Saltsjön, and ferried people out to Utö in the summer.

Now, in winter, she has been transformed into a floating Christmas *smörgåsbord,* with fully booked two-hour excursions in to Lake Mälar – two hours being the time it takes to get through the meal.

The entire after saloon is filled with delicacies: two tables of assorted herring dishes, one to port and one to starboard. A huge table in the centre, with Christmas fare, and a few small side tables with nuts and dates.

But there is no stampede, no crowding as on the boats to Finland.

The passengers are lunch with reverence; this is a unique ship, a real steamer, with a genuine compound engine whose unhurried piston movements are generated through the vessel like the heartbeats of a man who is in the best of shape, a stranger to stress.

Captain Torbjörn Svensson is proud of her. It is a miracle, of course, that she has survived, and is still afloat. But the Björkfjärden is still a relatively young steamer; built in 1925 she's never been involved in a collision, never sunk, and never caught fire, apart from a minor conflagration in the dining-room back in the 50s.

It was the Strömma Canal Company that saved her from the scrapyard in 1970, buying her at a compulsory auction. Torbjörn and the rest of the crew took her over in 1977.

Torbjörn's father, artist Roland Svensson, produced a series of steamer lithographs, the proceeds of which enabled the Björkfjärden to be refitted.

These are classical waters. Our attention is drawn to *"Brännvin"* Smitt's old mansion. Smitt, the Aquavit King, used to arrange *brännvin* trips out in this direction, as he did to islands off Djurgården.

"That little place there was once an inn, where Bellman wrote 'Card Game at the Club'!"

And *"brännvin* trips" were arranged to that, too. In fact most of what has been written about Lake Mälar is concerned with food and *brännvin,* or snaps. Karl Jonas Love Almqvist wrote his first *novell,* or long short story, in 1839. It starts on board the steamer Mariefred, and the entire description of the voyage is concerned with what they eat and drink on board.

This is the last trip on Lake Mälar for the year. The ice is already thick, and putting a strain on the steamer's plates. "She drinks an extra 40 litres of oil an hour in the ice," says Torbjörn.

"We'll just stop for a moment and take a postcard," he then announces over the loudspeaker.

And as the passengers get on with their meal, the crew climb out onto the ice. "There's never been a picture taken like this before," says Torbjörn. "They're a great crew. And she's a great boat!"

Lars Westman

The cook, with several days' supplies of breaded hams for the Björkfjärden's Yuletide Table.

*The Yuletide Table in the after saloon, and an
interior from the main dining-room (right).*

Crew members check the thickness of the ice, and decide to make this the last trip of the season.

Right: Torbjörn, the skipper, and his entire crew on the ice near Drottningholm Palace.

This is a real steam engine!

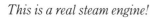

THE WINTER ICE

Every morning I went to the same observation post to observe how the long winter came and went–the built-in overhead platform connecting the Gondolen restaurant with the Katarina Elevator. The first sign of winter was when one of the icebreakers–Ymer or Frej, I don't recall which–put out from Stadsgården. It was an incredibly mild day in November, with a pale sun that almost deceived people into expecting an "Indian summer". Its destination, however, was the upper reaches of the Gulf of Bothnia, where ice, according to reports, had already started to form.

From where I stood, it was some time around the middle of December before any sign of ice was evident in Riddarfjärden. A tentative experiment, simply, a thin, shiny skin that yielded to the first northwester. But by now the water had been thoroughly and vaporously chilled, so that in January, when the wind next dropped, the

sheet of ice was there again, crossed by a narrow channel of open water from Västerbron in towards the Karl Johan lock. The shipping appeared now to be in a hurry to escape from the more rapidly freezing waters of Lake Mälar, while there was still time.

I imagined that there would be time enough to go down to Söder Mälarstrand, to the pub on the barge, and the youth hostel, and strap on my long-distance ice-skates. But the snow then fell in masses, and the temperature dropped still further. In spite of the snow cover, the ice must have thickened from below, because suddenly human tracks were clearly visible out on the areas south of the City Hall. The footprints made by bold commuters between Kungsholmen, Riddarholmen and Södermalm, who avoid in this way the crowded Underground stops all the way from Fridhemsplan to Zinkensdamm.

I could observe through my glasses some mornings how certain of these ice-walkers had stopped, leaning forward in their tracks. Was it really so cold, I wondered, that these poor souls had been transformed, from one instant to the next, into pillars of ice?

Only by a very fine adjustment of the lenses could I see, through the gusting snow, how the right hands of these figures out near Långholmen were performing regular jerks: these were winter-hardened "jiggers", fishing through the ice.

While the ice thus extended its empire westwards, the waters immediately below me, as I stood by the Katarina Elevator, were still black, and cavernously open. I glimpsed occasionally, beyond the bridge between Skeppsholmen and Kastellholmen, the fishermen of Ornö and their trawlers coming in to sell their catch at the quay in Nybroviken. Röda Bolaget's red tugs, Bull, Axel and little Ivar were now casting off less and less often from Stadsgården and the pontoon bridges off Slussen, on mysterious missions beyond the outermost point of Djurgården. Possibly there was a panic on in Värta harbour:

cont'd page 131

The Djurgården ferry in front of Kastellholmen.

Christmas trees being sold "in the old fashioned way", from one of the island boats.

Fishermen from Ornö at Nybroviken, selling fish caught during the night.

Theatre manager Per Edström clearing snow from the entrance to the Arena, the archipelago's floating theatre. Here moored at the quay near the Royal Dramatic Theatre.

I remembered vaguely an appeal for extra stevedores on the local radio. Perhaps the freight carriers were afraid that the ice would soon tighten its grip also on the approaches. But I could still see, one afternoon around three, two windsurfers picking up speed off Beckholmen, even as four skiers emerged from the bay at Rålambshov, and began to pole their way along the northern shore.

And so it went on until mid-February, with snow drifts from low clouds. Then, suddenly, we were hit for four consecutive days by temperatures of around fifteen degrees below. Up on the lift platform, the huge neon temperature readings flashed out by Philips were right behind me. The barometer was also unusually high. But the Philips engineers were wrong about the sun, which was in fact invisible, obscured by the smoky, slowly drifting ice-vapour that also blanketed the water surface below.

When the vapour finally dispersed, ice floes were to be seen drifting; only the few boats still in operation prevented the entire surface from being transformed into a single shore-to-shore carpet of ice. *cont'd page 135*

There's a white duck in Nybroviken. It's been there for several years.

Children believe it to be an enchanted prince (some children still do believe such things). Some adults believe it to be an albino duck, but it does not have the red eyes of the albino.

It is fatter than other ducks, because everyone wants to feed it, in the belief that it has a hard time because it is different.

In fact, the other ducks treat their white brother with great respect, and in no way reject him.

Or is it a she? For a whole week I saw this white duck swimming around with a female, the way ducks do when they have paired off for the season.

But when I came back the following week, the white duck had switched to a drake as companion. I threw some bread crumbs to the white duck, which surprisingly enough drew back and let the drake eat, as all living creatures do when they are thinking more about others than themselves.

It will soon be spring. And then the white duck will have to make up its mind!

Lars Westman

But one afternoon, in the early twilight, I detected certain promising signs. On the other side of the buoy south of Skeppsholmen, the ice seemed to have grown so thick that the swell could no longer eat away the ice cover closest to the shore. My decision was made: the following morning I would go skating on Strömmen! Something that has hardly been possible since the era of sail, when the harbour was completely closed in winter.

It was teeming with birds at dawn the following day as I marched with my ice pick, prods and casting line past the open, steaming waterhole below the Operakällaren Restaurant.

The frozen birds looked as if they would like to start clacking their beaks at me in unison, it was that icy cold.

"The last thing I want is to go down in this lot," I thought as I glided out on the nearest ice. Carefully I rounded, in a wide arc, some treacherous holes eaten in the ice by the current, in the passage between Blasieholmen and Skeppsholmen. The surface was sagging beneath me, and I dared not linger–I could hear from the sound that my weight was the absolute limit of what the ice would support. But by the time I reached the af Chapman things were better, I had to wield my pick several times to get a hole.

Hands behind my back, I set out along beside the central channel kept open by the Waxholm boats. The sound made by the contact between my skates and the midwinter ice was now entirely reassuring. Glancing to my left, towards Långa Raden, I saw some people standing and pointing. I supposed they had just caught sight of me.

I set course for the outermost point of Kastellholmen, where numerous blocks of ice were piled up. Still, I wondered if I couldn't get round these, and turn north up towards Strandvägen.

I never got that far. I heard a violent rustling in front of me, and up round the corner like a jack-in-the-box popped the day's first Djurgården ferry.

No time to lose, I had to retreat fast! With nasty little cracking sounds the tracks behind my fleeting steel heels broke open; as fast as I could, I spurted back towards the af Chapman.

Once again I was forced to change course. Behind the af Chapman's masts appeared the ice-breaking Skarpö, evilly churning up the channel, en route for Vaxholm and the archipelago. She was cutting straight towards my frozen path, as if the ice were melted butter. I veered hard starboard, to the safety of Skeppsholmen. There I was received by the same group of people as had recently observed with astonishment as I sailed proudly past in an east-south-easterly direction.

"Idiot," observed one of them, unpleasantly.

But so what, I thought to myself. I had just skated a good way across Strömmen. You don't do that every day. And today, I bet, the long winter would turn. From today the sun would climb to such warming heights that the ice-breaking vessels would no longer be needed–nor, for that matter, any ice-breaking skaters.

Soon we should be seeing these waters glittering and open once more.

Jan Sundfeldt